LIVING IN A FURRY SHADOW

HEATHER SMITH

SHORTLEAT PUBLICATIONS

Copyright 1997 Heather Smith

ISBN 0 9526039 2 6

First published by Shortleat Publications 1997

British Library Cataloguing in Publication Data. A catalogue record for this book is available from the British Library.

All rights reserved. No part of this publication may be reproduced, stored in a retrieval system, or transmitted, in any form or by any means, electronic, mechanical, photocopying, recording or otherwise, without permission of the publisher.

SHORTLEAT PUBLICATIONS

Published by Shortleat Publications, 5 Tresta Walk, Woking, Surrey, GU21 4XF

Printed by Arrow Offset, Padmores Yard, St John's Mews, St John's, Woking, Surrey, GU21 1ZE

Cover design and drawings by Jenny Whitmarsh

'A cat brings a soft-footed furry magic into your life and nothing will ever be quite the same again. So what could be better than one cat? Yes, of course! Two cats....or even three....or four....'

This book is dedicated to all victims of the 'furry magic' theory.

ALSO BY HEATHER SMITH

MALCOLM'S DIARY

MUCH MORE FROM MALCOLM

CONTENTS

Introduction.....Page 1
    Malcolm Moggs-Smythe sets the scene

Acknowledgements....Page 5

Days of Innocence and Unpicked Chairbacks....Page 7
    Life is calm and straightforward, but not for long

Breeds of Cat Owner....Page 13
    You might just recognise someone you know

And Fluffy Makes Three....Page 19
    Those blissful early days of cat ownership

So You Think You're Coping....Page 29
    Still besotted and getting worse

The Growing Family....Page 35
    Slippery slope time

The Naming of Cats....Page 41
    A new perspective on that all-important subject

Branching Out....Page 47
    Many are called and a few are foolish enough to answer

There are Furries at the Bottom of my Garden..Page 55
    The wilder side of cat rescue

Becoming an Expert....Page 61
    Who's kidding who?

Survival Strategies....Page 69
    Essential reading, even if you do feel it's too late

What Cats Think About Humans....Page 73
    Fluffy and her friends have their say

INTRODUCTION
BY MALCOLM MOGGS-SMYTHE

My devoted readers will understand why I anguished for some time before agreeing to provide an introduction to the Earth Mother's first solo attempt at authorship. For the whole of ten minutes, in fact, which was the time it took her to open a tin of sardines, find a plaster for her fingers and dollop them (the sardines, not her fingers) on to my plate. Principles are all very well, but a chap must keep body and soul together.

Naturally, I have been under a great deal of stress since joining the Earth Mother's household. There is a time for sleeping and a time for flogging yourself, and I suddenly knew I should heed my consultant's advice and slow down a bit. What he actually said was, 'More exercise and smaller portions would soon have the old devil looking more like a cat,' but I think he understood. After all, the poor man has had his own problems with you-know-who.

Anyway, here I am - the same sleek, handsome chap I've always been, but with a more relaxed, happy-go-lucky approach to life. For goodness' sake! Whatever is the woman doing? Oh, it's only an El Plonko bottle hitting the deck. For a moment I thought it was my Tom Kitten bowl.

As I was saying, I'm much more relaxed now and I even do a few little part-time jobs to keep the old brain cells jumping around. Yes, I still like to get up early and

Malcolm in retirement

have always finished breakfast by the time the postman comes. Then I go back to bed till around 11. No point in rushing at things.

Sometimes I do some food tasting to help the old Earth Mother out, because it would be extremely inconvenient if she were to take to her bed. Unfortunately, you often can't be sure until you're pretty well down to the last couple of mouthfuls. I don't mind, but it's no good expecting gratitude. Then on a pleasant afternoon I might assist the neighbours by testing their car brakes, but you have to be a bit selective. I wouldn't, for example, go skipping diagonally across the road in front of a Skoda, and I wouldn't chance it with the Earth Mother, even if she was driving a steam roller.

Now, they do say that imitation is the sincerest form of flattery and I wouldn't want anybody to think that I haven't done everything in my power to encourage the Earth Mother to cultivate her talents, meagre though they are. Some days I've allowed her to sit at the wordprocessor for a whole ten minutes before I've started screaming for food, but it's not appreciated. I often think it's a pity that the Earth Mother can't accept that all artists need to be put under a bit of pressure to give of their best instead of making that ridiculous fuss when I vomited up a furball all over Chapter 3.

Modesty prevents me from highlighting my own vital role in this enterprise, but Moggs-Smythe groupies will no doubt spot the odd velvet-pawed intervention here and there, not to mention the occasional pilchardy dribble in the margin. Once again, Auntie Jenny has done her stuff with the drawings, but I have to say that she has again flattered the Earth Mother. Fear is such a powerful motivator.

Whatever you do, don't take this book too seriously and don't start wondering if it's true. Of course it isn't – the reality is far more terrifying!

Malcolm Moggs-Smythe

ACKNOWLEDGEMENTS

I am, of course, more than grateful to dear Malcolm for his supportive introduction. If he hadn't been neutered some years previously, he soon would have been after that.

This book is inspired by the people and cats I have met over the years. The cats have all been wonderful; as for the humans, there have been a few 'ghastlies', but the balance has been more than restored by the sort of folk who think nothing of turfing out in all weathers to feed colonies of wild cats, or rushing an injured animal to the vet's in the deeply depressing hours of a winter's dawn.

My grateful thanks go to all the wonderful friends I have made through The Cats Protection League, and from writing 'Malcolm's Diary' and 'Much More From Malcolm'. I am afraid this book is their fault because their enthusiastic response – once I had recovered from the shock – encouraged me to go on writing.

Finally, I must thank Jenny Whitmarsh for her super drawings – and for putting up with me along the way.

Heather Smith

CHAPTER ONE

DAYS OF INNOCENCE AND UNPICKED CHAIRBACKS

The carpet tufts are of uniform length. The backs of the chairs are unmarked and no desiccated furball lurks on the tapestry cushions. The wallpaper adheres unerringly to the walls instead of snaking across the floor in forlorn scrolls; there are no pawprints on the tablecloth, and the food on the table appears to be intact.

This apparently idyllic state of affairs is about to change. It is hard to pinpoint the moment when the inhabitants begin to experience a strange emptiness – a feeling that their lives are somehow incomplete. It may have started on that holiday in Greece when a half-starved shadow stole on to the balcony and stuffed down the remains of the lamb kebabs..........or perhaps it was the girl in the office's fault for showing 1051 pictures of her new kitten before coffee?

This is a difficult and vulnerable time. Will they come to their senses before it's too late? Will they heed the dreadful warnings imparted by Mrs. Grimblethorpe down the road, or don't they care that her German Shepherd Dog was reduced to a quivering wreck by Tilley the Tortie, or that Big Ginger caught and consumed half-a-dozen Koi Carp *and still ate his breakfast?*

The answer is that of course they won't. Every single human trembling on the brink of cat ownership is convinced that this time it will be different. Not for them the ruined carpets, ripped open cushions or sleepless nights endured by weaker-minded cat owners. They will start as they mean to go on. Their lives will still be their own and if they want to go out for the evening, they'll go without any of this guilt rubbish about Kitty being left on her own. It would just be quite pleasant and cosy to have something warm and furry around the place and cats are undemanding pets – surely they've read that somewhere?

It is often the female half of a partnership who will come over all broody, leaving the male to counter these emotional excesses with sound, commonsense arguments. He will often laugh – not unkindly – as she gathers together a collection of cutie-pie cat ornaments; he might even indulge her by buying the odd winsome picture. After a few tearful interludes, he might even consider letting her have the kitten she's already arranged to collect from a friend the following day. After all, what could Mr Macho Man possibly have to fear from a few ounces of fur and whiskers? The answer, of course, is just about everything. Forget about sideshows like being born and getting married. Having a cat is the thing that really changes your life – if you still have one, that is!

The less enthusiastic member of the household may be forgiven for wondering whether the new arrival really neeeds a duvet with pawprints on one side and mice on the other, and for considering that three scratching posts and fifteen assorted food bowls might well be excessive, but by the time that preparations have reached their zenith he will be well acquainted with every petshop within a fifty-mile radius. Both humans will be well equipped to debate into the small hours the clumping properties of cat litter, or to appear on 'Mastermind' answering questions on flea treatments in the late 1990s. They will have emptied the library shelves of cat-care volumes and purchased a further fifty titles, each of which will inevitably contradict the advice given in the other forty-nine.

Much lively discussion will have taken place on the respective merits of male and female cats, with lists of names brandished whenever there happens to be a lull in the conversation. Friends and relatives will be sucked into the unending discussion and the more naive among them may even make the mistake of contributing a view.

As the obsession with having a cat or kitten gathers momentum, the prospective owners may flirt with the idea of a pedigree and trudge around countless cat shows to consider the relative advantages of Burmillas, Rag Dolls and Maine Coons. In most cases, however, there is a moggy waiting in the wings, just waiting for them to stop being silly and realise that he is the one for them.

A friend of mine once stipulated to her husband that she didn't mind what colour kitten she had as long as it wasn't black. He duly scampered off to view a kitten on the other side of town, returning empty handed. 'Well,' she demanded impatiently, 'where is it?' 'They only had a black one,' he explained patiently, whereupon she burst into tears and vowed she would never speak to him again if he didn't get back there pretty smartish and bring little Sooty home. I relate this sorry tale merely to illustrate that feelings can run high at such times, and one is not always at one's most logical.

An Egyptian moggy recognising a soft touch

If opposition remains a problem, help can sometimes come from unexpected quarters. Cats are experts at wheedling their way into human affections, as any reader of this book will no doubt realise and a co-operative neighbour's cat will often help to overcome any lingering resistance to the concept of cat ownership. A common technique is to strike up a friendship in the garden with the feline visitor showing a flattering interest in the gardener's project. This will continue until the gardener has come to enjoy the cat's company, when Puss will abruptly withdraw, leaving a puzzled and rather hurt human wondering what he's done wrong. By then, this sorry creature will be ready to fling open the door to any passing moggy and greet it like a long lost friend.

Of course, a successful survivor like the cat hasn't got where it has today without employing some pretty sophisticated home-locating techniques. It is a sobering thought that the one-eyed, cauliflower-eared tabby of uncertain vintage under a bush in Leeds is following in a noble tradition when he tunes into news of a vacancy for a small ginger kitten in the Isle of Wight. Never mind the details – the cat's ability to cut through irrelevancies and take the strategic view has stood it in good stead since an Egyptian moggy first clocked the potential of taking a position in a granary store.

Yes, sooner or later a travel-weary cat with a Northern accent will stroll through a door in Ventnor; even stranger to report, the humans will feel honoured and will clasp the creature to their collective bosom. And it's a nice thought that only a few centuries and a few civilisations separate them from the ancient Egyptian who once shared his lunch with a rather elegant creature that may or may not have sported a cauliflower ear, but certainly knew a soft touch when it saw one.

CHAPTER TWO

BREEDS OF CAT OWNER

Even if you happen to be one of those strange humans who is not captivated by cats, a study of the different types of cat owner may provide some satisfaction, not to mention a less than attractive sense of superiority. The following descriptions summarise the types most frequently encountered by anyone who spends any amount of time homing cats and kittens.

THE BUSINESSLIKE BRIGADE

This group likes to feel in charge of things and sets about organising every aspect of its life with a vigour that the more muddled amongst us find absolutely terrifying.

These folk will have identified the exact moment when the new cat or kitten should make an appearance. An hour beforehand will find them at the dentist; an hour later they will be rushing off to the hairdresser. They can be relied upon to have purchased everything needed, including litter tray liners and kitty lit deodorisers, and will have a very clear idea of the sort of feline they require.

They will cling to the belief that somewhere there exists a cat that will consider it an honour to fit in with their very important and pressurised lives. In their wilder dreams they imagine that there are cats that actually care whether or not their owners get to work on time, and worry if they leave the house with something very nasty adhering to their clothing. Although it defies belief, this group actually believes – in the early stages of cat ownership – that their cat will co-operate when they are in a hurry to get it to the vet or the cattery, instead of wandering around the woods high on catnip. This group is in for some major disappointments.

SOFT TOUCHERS

These people often present as reasonably rational beings, but a couple of minutes' observation of their reactions to a poster depicting a kitten with a bandage on its paw will reveal all. These are the folk that know perfectly well they should choose the bright, forward kitten , but inevitably go home with the trembling, weepy-eyed one that is half the size of the rest of the litter. They will be back, of course – not to complain, but to collect the kitten's mother, particularly if she happens to have one eye.

Although this group appears to be living in cloud cuckoo land, it is actually a lot closer to reality than the first group. Soft touchers harbour no theories about the new arrival fitting in with their lifestyle: they know only too well that they stand as much chance of being the boss with a cat in the house as a giant squid stands of winning the Monaco Grand Prix.

FATALISTS

Although their are some sophisticated variations on this particular theme, the guiding principle for this group is that sooner or later a cat will just turn up. They will then know that they were 'meant to have it', and that in

The Businesslike Brigade expect the cat to co-operate when they are in a hurry, instead of ignoring them

some strange way this means they cannot be held responsible for their actions. Sometimes, of course, a reluctant cat owner may not be above subscribing to this philosophy in the naive and doomed belief that the evil moment may be postponed indefinitely.

These sad souls have reckoned without the powers of the cat in Leeds and his relations. It would certainly be advisable to keep a close eye on the garden path before indulging in a self-congratulatory grin.

SENTIMENTALISTS

These are the people who are seeking a very specific type of cat – one that looks and behaves just like the cat they knew and loved and have recently lost. They will search high and low, armed with fistfuls of photographs of the departed and will openly despair of ever finding a cat or kitten they could love as they loved Saint Fluffy.

The endearing thing about these folk is that having scoured the land for a longhaired ginger boy with a white patch over his left eye, they will suddenly succumb to the charms of a spiteful black female with hardly any fur and will love her with a passion that takes everybody by surprise, including the cat.

THE GHASTLIES

These are the people that should never have so much as a dead rat, never mind a cat. Their perception of cat ownership is of the 'grab it, play with it, chuck it out' variety and they are to be found in every corner of society. They are generally accompanied by mini-ghastlies who have learnt that it is a jolly thing to swing a kitten by its tail or shut it in a cupboard for hours on end. They will want the kitten *immediately,* will have given absolutely no consideration to its needs and will be full of righteous indignation when it soils the carpet even though no dirt tray has been provided.

The disheartening thing is that sooner or later they will obtain a kitten, which will later be handed to a rescue organisation if it's lucky, or dumped on the M25 if it isn't.

Call me an old misery - and it has been known - but I am convinced it is all too easy for people to acquire animals, without having thought things through to the point where they are fully committed to the idea. Quite how this can be resolved I'm not sure, but putting a stop to the sale of cats and kittens in pet shops would be an extremely effective start. Charging a lot of money for an animal does nothing to ensure its happiness, but some hard talking about the level of care required and a general raising of awareness levels just might. Although there are, no doubt, some excellent pet shops that do all the right things, there are also some hell holes which are concerned with one thing only - a quick and substantial profit, with the wellbeing of the hapless animal somewhere below the till rolls in priority terms.

SHOPPING LIST.

For Fluffy
- CAT LITTER
- KITTY-DINS - KITTEN FOOD
- PING PONG BALLS
- PINK MOUSE
- BLUE MOUSE
- SCRATCHING POST
- CAT NIP
- FLEA STUFF
- WORM STUFF
- CHICKEN
- SALMON

For us
- BAKED BEANS
- BREAD
- EL PLONKO (LARGE)

CHAPTER THREE

AND FLUFFY MAKES THREE

We shall focus now on those joyful early days of cat ownership and follow the fortunes of the delighted humans as they get to know the new arrival. There is no question about it – these people are soft touchers. They may have started off as members of the Businesslike Brigade, or Fatalists, but they are now fully paid up members of the Soft Touchers Society. They may at some future date become Sentimentalists, but one thing is certain: they never have been and never will be Ghastlies.

Quite apart from the heady excitement brought on by deciding which type of cat litter to buy, the first time cat owner – or the owner who has not introduced a new cat or kitten for some years – is likely to experience a range of thrills and spills which would make an outing to Disneyland seem pretty tame.

If they have chosen a kitten, they are almost certain to suffer from Disappearing Kitten Syndrome (DKS) at an early stage. Although they will have noticed that Fluffy is very small indeed, the chances are that they will have failed to notice just how small. After being the centre of attention for a few hours, Fluffy is likely to get the hump when her humans start attending to some trifling needs like sleeping or eating; this is precisely when DKS strikes.

Suddenly the humans will become uneasily aware that

Fluffy hasn't been seen for some time. They will adopt a frivolous approach at first, going round the house making silly squeaky kissy noises and noisily vowing to let Fluffy come out in her own time. No sooner will they have resolved to leave the kitten to her own devices than they will start to ransack the house, ripping off cupboard doors and dismantling washing machines and fridges.

In the case of couples the strain will tell within a remarkably short period of time. Forget any romantic notions about pulling together in adversity; each is sure to blame the other for Fluffy's disappearance and a whole barrage of emotional shrapnel will be flying around, including dark references to his mother and her father.

After about three hours communications will have all but ceased, apart from the occasional dispirited tapping of Fluffy's bowl. The male human will have succumbed to melancholia by this stage and is likely to be discovered seated on the settee fondling Fluffy's baby mousey until his reverie is interrupted by the sound of sobbing. Wearily he wends his way upstairs to find his partner laughing and crying simultaneously as she hugs a rather cross-looking kitten. 'She was asleep in the dressing table drawer,' she sobs. The man is made of sterner stuff. Yes, he's pleased the kitten's been found, but there's no chance of him bursting into tears. He just happens to have a bit of a cold, that's all.

Suddenly life is worth living again and one small kitten has taken the first tottering step towards establishing total control over her human family. The clearer the warning signs, the more certain it is that they will be totally – and disastrously – ignored.

And it's not just kittens that manage to disappear. Adult cats, although considerably bulkier, are extremely skilled — not merely at hiding away, but in escaping from a hermetically sealed room or pen.

A cat named Tuppence came to stay with me last summer while his doting owners nipped off to Cornwall for a week. Having waved them off with bland assurances that they mustn't worry about their boy, I popped out to the cat pen to see how young Tuppence was settling in. The only snag was that he didn't seem to be in there. For some moments my mind wouldn't accept that the pen was empty, and it was only after I'd snatched up the blankets several times and double checked the roof that I at last noticed a neat round hole in the wire.

If only I'd noticed that he had concealed a pair of wirecutters under his smart black and white coat! In the space of no more than five minutes our hero had bitten through the wire and departed without so much as a farewell note. Luckily, having gained his freedom, Tuppence's concentration began to falter and he couldn't quite think why he'd gone to all that trouble. He was soon discovered strolling round next door's garden and gave himself up without a struggle.

One poor soul who two days previously had taken on a particularly neurotic tortoiseshell phoned me in floods of tears to inform me that the cat had escaped through the letterbox. Now cats are pretty sneaky, but through *the letterbox*? No doubt the cat in question was listening in to the conversation from the depths of the wardrobe or some other cosy hiding place, with its paw clamped across its mouth and its shoulders shaking, because it emerged minutes later yawning and stretching in an exaggerated manner.

Of course, for some cats escaping from a house or cat pen does not quite satisfy their craving for excitement. Such pussycats are tireless in their search for new thrills and spills and it's not always the obvious tearaways that give the most trouble. Beware in particular the cosseted pet that is not used to being hauled off by a total stranger. It is likely that little Mitzi or Boris or Mugwallop will have been placed in his or her pretty little wicker basket by the besotted owner.

Initially the cat will sit as if carved in stone, looking neither left nor right. All will be well until the vehicle transporting pussy is batting along at 50 or 60 mph, when Mitzi will squeeze her pretty little head between the door of the basket and the ancient wickerwork before flying through the air to land with a triumphant scrabble on the driver's chest. As the car swerves violently towards the opposite side of the road and back again, the driver's excitement is likely to be enhanced by the companionable tooting and waving of fellow road users.

Having survived a few minor dramas, the new owner may feel encouraged to attempt the assault course known as taking Kitty to the vet's.

Kittens are easy – you just scoop them up and pop them into the cat carrier. So far, so good. Unfortunately, a complacent human is a real challenge to a kitten and to assume that something so small is helpless is always a grave mistake. A resourceful kitten has a whole repertoire of set pieces at its disposal, of which choking is merely for starters.

A hitherto unexplained mystery is the ability of kittens to produce copious amounts of diarrhoea even though they haven't eaten for hours and had apparently emptied their bowels before beginning the journey. The experienced owner will ignore this sort of thing, having developed a resistance to obnoxious smells over the years and being confident that nothing is likely to reduce the time spent in the waiting room quite so effectively as a whiffy kitten.

The new owner, however, is inclined to panic and will make every effort to clean the kitten up while lurching along a dual carriageway. This is not to be recommended; even if a custodial sentence is avoided, the removal of kitten-pooh from most fabrics is a tricky business.

The kitten still has a few tricks up its fur, including screaming which can reduce the most resilient adult to tears after prolonged exposure. A particularly effective ploy is to scream nonstop for ten minutes or so, then go silent. Not many owners can resist the temptation to check whether Kitty is still in the land of the living. And you thought all those drivers were wearing Russian hats!

Adult cats do all of the above, but to a greater extent. In addition, the very sight of a cat basket is enough to produce rabid behaviour in the most placid of felines. Some cats like to sleep in their carrying basket, but you can bet your life that if you are actually intending to transport Fluffy to the vet's, you will be confronted with more teeth and claws than were featured in the whole of 'Jurassic Park'.

Assuming the intrepid humans eventually succeed in flushing Fluffy out from under the bed, or in dragging her down from the wardrobe without breaking their necks, and assuming that desperation will have given them the strength to ram her into the basket, there is still much to be endured. Even if they survive the journey, complete with piddling, poohing and panic, the waiting room with all its horrors looms ahead.

Apart from screaming and looking so terrified that everyone imagines poor Kitty has been beaten to within an inch of her life, there is still further scope for embarrassment. There is, for example, the probing muzzle of Freddie, the friendly Basset. It is a sad thing that cats rarely reciprocate the enthusiasm exhibited by dogs in vets' waiting rooms, and an even sadder thing that dogs do not look their best with their ears shredded. Even if the Freddies of this world have behaved in a foolish and forward manner, their owners can be slow to see the joke.

Once inside the surgery, the mature cat's owner will wish to unburden himself by telling the vet what a dreadful time he's had with Fluffy, and will suggest that the vet dons gauntlets and face mask before confronting the wild beast. The vet will smile in a kindly way as he reaches into the carrier, while the owner clings to the table, knuckles all but through the skin. This is Fluffy's cue to behave like a little furry angel, twinkling sweetly at the vet and throwing scornful glances at her owner.

The vet will helpfully show the owner how to administer Fluffy's worm pills, pointing out that a calm owner invariably produces a calm cat as if he had a vested interest in pushing the poor soul over the brink.

Experienced cat people will always be able to tell whether the cat in a particular home has required medication. There will be a sad collection of recently opened tins, each more expensive than the one before, and an even sadder heap of shredded towels. On the blood-smeared note by the telephone will be the GP's phone number and the location of the nearest Casualty Department, and looking ten years older than they did at the beginning of this eventful day will be the proud owners of Fluffy, the suburban tiger.

Far from causing a rift in the relationship between Fluffy and her owners, such battles actually appear to encourage bonding. It is not at all unusual to find City executives in sharp-looking suits boasting about their war wounds in smart crowded winebars; there is a strange sort of pride which springs from opening your heart to a wild beast - even if it's a wild beast which doubles as a hot water bottle on chilly nights.

In the carefree, cat-free days holidays were contemplated with joyful anticipation. Days were ticked off, brochures thumbed through, suntan lotion and beachwear purchased with unalloyed excitement. So what has changed? Why is there a feeling of dread rather than anticipation whenever anybody mentions Majorca, Marbella or Madagascar? Could it possibly be that 4kg of furry malevolence is to blame? Of course it is.

When they return from that guilt-ridden trip, they are destined to pay a terrible price for every sun-soaked moment

Every care has been taken over Fluffy's holiday arrangements, but a number of worries remain. Will she starve herself to death? Will she escape from the cattery? Will she forget all about Mummy and Daddy?

In vain will others seek to reassure because 'others' cannot compete with Fluffy when it comes to emotional blackmail. It is certain that as her humans leave the cattery, their last memories of Fluffy will be of a small furry body pressed up against the wire, screaming its head off. What they would never believe is that ten minutes later, Fluffy will either have her head in the trough or be busy ogling Big Butch in the adjacent pen.

When they return from their guilt-ridden trip, they are destined to pay a terrible price for every sun-soaked moment. For a start, Fluffy won't recognise them and will shrink into her bed when they come to collect her. She will cling pathetically to the blanket as they struggle to reassure her and brace herself against the door of the carrier. Once home, she will refuse to speak, shooting out of the house at the first opportunity and staying out all night so that their jet lag is compounded by another sleepless night. The following night, Fluffy will shower them with affection, purring and padding into the early hours.

The final act of revenge will be to piddle in the suitcase, hoping that by the time this is noticed, irreversible damage will have been done to contents and case. Even better, the sabotage might not be noticed until next year - what a jolly jape that would be!

Sadly, even this yobbish behaviour is likely to be tolerated by Fluffy's owners because apparently it shows how much she missed them. It really makes you wonder if the old Evolution Theory holds up, doesn't it?

CHAPTER FOUR

SO YOU THINK YOU'RE COPING?

At some stage in the process of cat ownership, the humans are certain to feel on top of things. This may happen early on, possibly when the first kitten pooh has landed in the dirt tray rather than on the coconut matting, or it may be later when Kitty appears to have swallowed her worm pill. These are dangerous moments, because at the first sign of complacency the cat is programmed to go into disaster mode. They have an impressive selection of crises to draw on and the following examples do no more than scratch the surface of feline inventiveness.

Sudden Illness at Awkward Moments

Mention within the hearing of a cat (a radius of some three thousand miles) that a holiday, an important business trip or a dinner party is planned and you might as well book an appointment at the vet's at the same time. Except, of course, the little treasure will not be taken ill during surgery hours. Ten minutes before departure, or before the guests are due to arrive, Kitty will mope about a bit, causing her distracted owner to snap, 'Now don't you come that old hang-cat look with me, Kitty. I know there's nothing wrong with you and that's that.'

The purpose of 'le grand mope' is twofold. Kitty, out of the kindness of her little furry heart is giving her owners a last chance to make amends and abandon any plans for a fun time; the second objective is to make them feel guilty for the rest of their lives because they failed to take Kitty's symptoms seriously.

Nobody has ever satisfactorily explained how it is that a cat or kitten that is chasing ping pong balls all over the house one minute can manage to lose half its bodyweight and be salivating heavily with one eyelid closed the next time you look at it. One thing we do know, however, is that the consequences are inevitable. Flights will be cancelled, job prospects jeopardised and friends alienated. Once at the specially opened surgery, Kitty will gulp bravely and do her best to open her eye/put the injured foot to the ground/swallow without wincing with pain. Even more amazing, by the time the owner is reading the small print on the travel insurance policy, or extinguishing the flames around the Beef Wellington, plucky little Kitty may even be playing with her ping pong ball again.

Disappearance

Cats are sensitive creatures and nothing upsets them so much as the feeling that their owners are in a hurry and that they may not be top priority at that particular moment. Imagine it – Fluffy has been in a fever of excitement all day, waiting for her owners to come home so that she can tell them about the leaf falling into the pond, then in they swoop, fling out half a tin of Kittydins, and dive into the shower without so much as a civil word.

A particular skill that felines have perfected over the years is the ability to be 'not quite visible'. This means that the humans in the household are unable to agree exactly when Fluffy was last seen. OK, there was a shadowy sort of cat in the drive when they arrived home, but thinking about it now they really couldn't be sure it was Fluffy. It could so easily have been Mugwump from number three, or Tiddles from the bungalow...

Gradually, tension will escalate with everybody finally being convinced that Fluffy has been missing for days.

A thorough search of the house and garden will naturally prove unsuccessful, usually culminating in spiteful remarks being made and relationships plummeting to an all-time low. 'Of course I love Fluffy more than you,' can take a bit of getting over.

The plunging of owners into perilous situations also gives Fluffy a good laugh. I well remember searching in the woods for my much-loved ginger cat, Thomas. In the fitful beam of the torch, for it was a foul winter's night, I caught sight of a sinister looking man some way off of the main footpath. Instead of wondering what the hell he was up to, having no dog about his person, I grilled him about my lost cat, only to discover that he was French. Not having a clue what ginger might be in French, I decided that 'red' would have to do. 'Avez-vous vu un chat rouge?' I enquired animatedly, but I was never to know whether he had or not because he shot off into the bushes at the gallop. Needless to say, young Thomas was waiting on the doorstep when I finally returned home, none too pleased about the delay over his tea.

Embarrassment
Cats are the undisputed champions in this field. Stuff a pair of knickers into the washing machine and fail to shut the door properly, and Buster will present them to that rather prim young man from the insurance company next time he calls. Spend hours trying to track down the hindquarters of the mouse whose head and forelimbs you discovered on the work-top and Kitty will find them as your mother-in-law walks through the door.

There is nothing more tiresome than trying to intercept the hunt as it stampedes through the strawberry pavlova

Cats are also capable of a more sophisticated level of embarrassing behaviour. A neighbour of mine placed his property on the market but didn't want the immediate neighbours to be aware of this at an early stage. Unfortunately, when the estate agent took the photograph - which subsequently appeared in every local paper - my very distinctive grey and white cat, Malcolm, was sitting on his drive. Oops.

Bringing Home Friends

If her people seem to be coping rather well with everything else she has thrown at them, Kitty will often feel the need to extend her repertoire by importing desirable creatures from the wilderness beyond the dustbin.

The experienced cat owner will naturally ensure that all windows and pussyflaps are firmly battened down when friends call, there being nothing more tiresome than trying to intercept the hunt as it stampedes through the strawberry pavlova. The less seasoned owner, however, may still be suffering under the delusion that Puss is bringing them a present. Forget what the animal psychologists say - Puss simply has an overdeveloped sense of humour.

Even those of us who have lived in a furry shadow for years can still be caught off guard. When flinging open the broom cupboard recently, I foolishly ignored the bright-eyed presence at my side and grabbed the carpet sweeper to reveal a tightly coiled grassnake dozing the afternoon away. Seconds later I was trying to separate snake and cat without actually passing out or being sick.

And it's not just feeble women who have problems with the creatures from the cauldron. Two bulky men who were supposed to be removing furniture from my bedroom suddenly and with one accord dashed from the room. The cause of their excitement? A mummified frog, clearly recognisable even under six inches of fur and fluff.

So the new owners have come through all these challenges and are still besotted with their pet. She has brought a soft-footed furry magic into their lives and nothing will ever be quite the same again. So what could be better than one cat? Yes, of course! Two cats....or even three......or four..........

CHAPTER FIVE

THE GROWING FAMILY

Having warmed to the idea, most people can't wait to acquire another cat. They will have convinced themselves that they are doing all this for Kitty because she is lonely, and will be beside herself with delight when the new arrival joins the household.

This is odd, because most of the owners are intelligent, well-adjusted folk who would certainly think twice about sticking their heads in a gas oven or leaping off Beachy Head, even on a fine day. Can they really have banished all the horror stories from their minds? What about the way Aunt Emily's Porky behaved when Sooty the kitten took up residence? It took years to get those stains out of the carpet. And what about Lucky when Mrs. Jones took in that stray tortoiseshell? I won't dwell on that unfortunate episode, but we must be grateful that Mrs. Jones was wearing her plastic raincoat at the time.

Nothing daunted, the humans will trip around, visiting sanctuaries and following up advertisements until they suddenly realise they cannot live without Susie, or Sammy, or Micheldever. The only snag is that this particular feline is one of a pair – a pair that cannot possibly be separated. An anguished discussion takes place, one party being unable to see any problems and the other being unable to see anything but. Is it really so different having three cats to having two? The logical answer to the question is a resounding 'yes', but for some reason logic carries no weight whatsoever in this situation.

Imagine Kitty's unbounded joy when she is presented with one or two new friends! How will she show her gratitude? The answer probably lurks within the following list of options:

- she may attempt to kill her new friends;

- she may attempt to kill her owners;

- she may ignore everybody and piddle on the mat;

- she may fall in love with one of the new arrivals and demand to have his kittens, even though this would take a biological miracle.

As with humans, there is no accounting for feline taste and it is likely that the more disreputable the cat, the more Kitty will dote on him. If he is covered with fleas and shedding tapeworm segments over the Laura Ashley furnishings, so much the better. One of my own treasures – the unbelievably neurotic and snobbish Princess Mildred– comes over quite unnecessary when she sees Saint Stripey, a battered tomcat of uncertain years, but cannot stand the sight of the inoffensive and squeaky clean Patch. It works the other way round as well. All the boy cats like Miss Bean – a strange little cat with a perpetually runny eye and bald ears – but can take or leave pretty, kittenish Lucy. There is hope for us all!

Most cats will settle down together after a few nerve-jangling weeks, but not until they have brought their humans to the brink of a breakdown or a divorce, or possibly both. Cats enjoy seeing their owners 'in a state' and it is very important to try to avoid giving them this

The more disreputable the cat, the more Kitty will dote on him

satisfaction. It is not at all unusual to find that cats are very much more aggressive with each other when their owners are around, partly no doubt through jealousy, but also because they enjoy seeing them at the end of their tether.

It actually is fascinating – and fun – to have more than one cat because the presence of a kindred spirit dramatically extends the feline repertoire in terms of both mental and physical activity. And there is always the consoling thought that how ever many cats you have, they will never gang up on their owners. Not because they don't want to, but because they would never be able to agree when, where or how this should be achieved.

The Introduction Process

For every introduction that goes without a hitch, there are at least a thousand that don't. Kittens are usually the easiest to introduce, proving once again (as if we didn't already know) that it's the old hormones that are the cause of all the trouble. Most kittens aren't particularly interested in being King of the Castle or Queen of the May, being much more fascinated by silver paper balls and feathers. There is generally no need to worry about bad language in kittens; it rarely leads to bloodshed, but it would be as well to monitor their television viewing more closely.

A few months and a few hormones further down the line and events are likely to take a very different turn. If the resident cat is a fairly relaxed sort of neutered boy, he may storm off into the night when the newcomer appears, but is likely to return within the hour shrugging his shoulders and pluckily resolving to make the best of it, particularly if the new cat is a girl. Let vets assure me that once they are neutered it makes no difference - I beg to differ. Girls are girls and boys are boys, and a few minor adjustments here and there don't alter the basic characteristics of the animal concerned. I am a firm believer in the 'opposites attract' theory, and have generally found that this holds good when increasing one's feline family.

Beware, however, the middle-aged female cat who has ruled the roost since kittenhood. Such a girlie is unlikely to see the fun of having her tail tweaked by a supercharged furry funpack, be it male or female. She is even less likely to be impressed by the sight of a younger, prettier female adult. A sycophantic toy boy is probably the best bet, as long as he doesn't have ideas above his station once his paws are under the table.

Dogs are often quite good about welcoming a new cat or kitten, but it is as well to make sure they're not thinking in terms of a tasty addition to the menu. Dogs tend to fall into two categories: the 'don't-let-it-hurt-me-I-only-want-to-be-friends' type, and the 'that-was-a-tasty-snack-I-wouldn't-mind-another' variety. Kittens are almost always brave with dogs - sometimes foolishly so - and must be protected from themselves. Adult cats that haven't been used to dogs usually end up with things organised the way they like them, so long as they're not having to cope with the Hound of the Baskervilles, and as long as the cat is of an outgoing and confident disposition. A nervous cat is unlikely to do well with dogs unless it has been used to them from an early age, and nervous owners are unlikely to do well with anything at all.

So now Kitty is contentedly sharing her home with at least one other feline and the owners – after several sleepless nights and lip-gnawing days – are beginning to feel that life could settle down and that at some point it might almost become enjoyable again. The cheerful little boy cat they imported to cheer Kitty up has suffered a few blows to the head, but is bearing up and has only been to the vet's once during the past five days. Kitty has decided not to starve herself to death after all and although the carpet has sustained major injuries, they never liked it anyway. Who said owning cats wasn't all milk and Kittydins?

CHAPTER SIX

THE NAMING OF CATS

Once a person's life has taken a decidedly catty turn, he or she is likely to spend a lot of time anguishing over the naming process. Sometimes, of course, a new arrival will already have a name which may or may not seem appropriate to the new owners. This presents them with a particularly tricky challenge as they will want to find a name that sounds similar to the original, while wishing to bestow a fitting title on their new pet. This accounts for some rather odd names, such as 'Cater', which started out as 'Katie'; the new owners then became aware of the cat's preoccupation with the kitchen and every aspect of food preparation............well, OK, it might seem a bit silly but the cat didn't mind.

Human Names
Much innocent amusement can be had as a result of giving a cat a human name, especially if you are talking to someone who doesn't realise you have a cat called Fred, or Sheila, or Nigel.

I have several cats with human names, not by design, but simply because I felt they couldn't be called anything else.

George, the macho tabby, is always causing trouble and it is unfortunate that a friend of mine has just acquired a boyfriend who appears to have been named after my cat. I also have a 'Lucy'. The other day in the office I was lamenting the fact that Lucy often gives me the slip when I would quite like to get her to the vet's. What I actually said was, 'I hope I'll be able to get hold of Lucy later on.' My long-suffering colleague, no doubt listening with half an ear, looked startled. 'You can't expect her to answer the phone, Heather. she's a *cat.*'

As readers will be all too aware, I also share my home with a rather overbearing grey and white cat called Malcolm, who has acquired a certain notoriety from his infamous Diaries. Imagine my reaction when the phone rang one Saturday morning and I was plunged into the following conversation:
Caller: Could I speak to Malcolm, please?
Me, thinking someone was having me on and that I'd soon realise who it was: I'm afraid he's gone out.
Caller: Oh, no! That's a bit of a problem. Do you know how long he's likely to be?
Me: I've no idea. He never tells me where he's going or how long he'll be, and I'm getting absolutely sick of it!
Caller, after an uneasy silence: Well, if he comes back in the next hour or so, could you ask him if he'd be free to play cricket this afternoon?

Yes, it was a complete stranger who'd got the wrong number. I explained, as best I could and, to the caller's eternal credit, he seemed to quit enjoy the mental picture of a large grey and white cat in full cricketing gear.

Themes

Once people get into the multi-cat business, they often think it's rather a stylish thing to have a theme. I know of a household which accommodates a Doodlebug

Malcolm settling down for a long innings

and a Zeppelin, and I have a feeling that a Spitfire may be joining them in the very near future. In another establishment, Poirot, Marple and Dalgleish reign supreme. Flowery names never lose their popularity, but this can be a problem with the boys, even if you go for something quite manly like Thistle or Burdock, and if a Daisy turns out to be more of a Davy you really have got problems.

Psychological Damage

Who knows what psychological damage is caused by calling boy cats by girls' names, to the owners as well as the cats? I can only say that I am personally acquainted with a Betty-Boy, who is one of the toughest, meanest cats I have ever met. Who can say whether being called Brutus from an early stage would have turned him into a tea-cosy?

Cats are also sensitive about their ages, and it is very important to bear this in mind when selecting a name. Imagine the embarrassment caused to a young-at-heart cat forced to answer to 'Elvis', or to a baby-faced girl when her owner yodels 'Cilla' over the back fence.

Commonly Occurring Surnames

Forget about Sooty, Tiger and Gismo. There is much more to a cat than its first name, as will become apparent after only the teeniest bit of eavesdropping as a cat-loving neighbour struggles to round up the furry family.

Many feline surnames seem to end in exclamation marks, as in Snowdrop You're-Letting-All-The-Heat-Out! and Stanislas Don't-Push-Your-Luck! The multi-barrelled effect is impressive, but for sheer simplicity Fluffy No! takes a lot of beating.

Then there are names that end in questionmarks, even though everybody - particularly the cat - will be well aware that no answer will be forthcoming - ever. Stripey Why-Do-You-Think-We've-Got-A-Pussyflap? is common in some parts, as is Reginald Couldn't-You-Have-Done-That-Outside? Theobald Why? retains its popularity whatever the state of the economy.

The third group of surnames consists of statements, generally invented by owners desperate to reassure themselves that they are in control, in spite of overwhelming evidence to the contrary. We therefore come across Cymbeline I-Know-What's-Best and Adolphus When-I-Say-No-I-Mean-No. Who are they kidding?

All of this could make life hideously complicated for cats when they married, but luckily they tend not to take their names very seriously and also rarely bother to go through with wedding arrangements. This fluid approach to naming makes life very difficult for the police. Even if someone recognised an Identikit picture of a feline villain, the police couldn't be sure whether they were looking for Sidney Will-You-Leave-That-Alone! or Sidney You've-Ripped-That-Dustbin-Bag-For-The-Last-Time.

Pet Names

And, of course, whatever name is bestowed on a cat, it is likely that a host of other names will be used in preference to his or her official title.

I had a dear cat years ago with the given name of Spooki, but to the end of her very long life we called her 'Baby' simply because in the early stages of her life here she happened to be the youngest of three. The fact that she then became the oldest of ten counted for nothing and she was still rejoicing in the name of 'Baby' on her 18th birthday, when with grizzled muzzle and stiff joints she tucked into a large plate of mashed prawns.

The origin of many pet names is inevitably lost in the mists of time and this may not be such a bad thing. When forced to confront such titles as 'Pooh Bot', 'Piddleshanks' and 'Legover', most of us wouldn't want to dwell on the event that sparked off such labelling, and whatever gave rise to the affectionate naming of 'Thunderballs' one can only surmise.

At least we needn't worry about the effect that all this has on cats since I have yet to come across the cat that takes a blind bit of notice of any name, unless the summons is accompanied by the promise of something pretty yummy and plenty of it.

CHAPTER SEVEN

BRANCHING OUT

Incredibly, many cat owners (obviously possessing marked masochistic tendencies) at some stage decide to become involved in cat rescue, although perhaps 'decide' isn't quite the right word if my own experience is anything to go by.

It was a Sunday afternoon - the sort of afternoon when a phone call from a double-glazing salesman would be a valuable source of excitement - when the phone actually did ring, in a rather muffled sort of way as it was having to make itself heard through a large furry body.

It was the Co-ordinator of a neighbouring Cats Protection League Branch, desperately ringing round to all Headquarters members to enlist their help. I made my smug little speech, about working full-time in London, having very few spare hours in the week, being unable to commit myself, etc., etc. I must admit that even to my own ears it all sounded pretty pathetic, and the fact that the caller was elderly and blind didn't help. Anyway, here I am some twelve years later, up to my elbows in pooh sacks and furballs, having resigned from a perfectly sensible job with an even more sensible salary.

Cats get under your skin, that's what happens, in a way that nobody can ever quite explain. It's not as if they're grateful, or even polite in some cases. Give a stray pink salmon and he's quite likely to infer that red would have been that bit tastier; mince up freshly cooked chicken and somebody is bound to wonder if it's free-range. None of this will stop them eating the food, of course, it's just that one is left with the uncomfortable feeling that one hasn't quite measured up.

Back to the blind lady. In common with all seasoned cat rescuers, she knew better than to dump twenty waifs and strays on me and head for the hills. Instead, it all started with a bit of gentle fundraising and lots of gratitude, so that I began to feel indispensable and hardly noticed the erosion of weekends and days off. This is not to imply any sneakiness on the part of the person seeking help: the neglect and ill-treatment of animals is such a desperate problem that I wouldn't blame anybody for marching 'volunteers' to car boot sales at gunpoint if they felt it would have the desired effect.

Some people - often those who have promised much at the outset - will inevitably melt away, leaving those who, while protesting that they couldn't possibly do anything else, are already eyeing up their back gardens to see where a cat pen or two could be accommodated. There then follows a mysterious happening, akin to the sudden appearance of crop circles, when the person who hadn't a minute to devote to cat rescue finds herself with a dozen cats to rehome and forgets that she ever had a more rational way of life.

To dwell for a moment on the subject of fundraising, it must be acknowledged that this is itself a complex activity worthy of study by anyone wishing to learn more about the darker side of human nature. The first thing that any student would notice is that fundraising for charity is – with certain notable exceptions – an almost exclusively female activity. When a man does appear, it is usually to explain how things could have been done more satisfactorily and instead of giving him a resounding slap the women will invariably dribble with gratitude and rush to provide him with a well-earned cup of coffee.

The student would also observe that there are basically two types of fundraiser. The first revels in the scrum of a car boot sale, the second prefers the more salubrious environment of a craft fair or coffee morning. Car boot sales are not for the fainthearted, including those who have strong views about complete strangers crawling all over their car or even over them. A willingness to employ vigorous language is an essential requirement, as regular car booters will inevitably consider you stuck up if you refuse to engage in some pretty spirited banter.

Craft fairs masquerade as more genteel affairs, but the same raw instincts prevail beneath the surface. Being clumsy is not an asset on these occasions as I have often found to my cost. Any slight excitement starts my arms windmilling and I never have the slightest idea what my bottom might be doing until I hear an expensive sounding crash from an adjacent stall.

We have been slow to recognise the moneymaking potential of the tried and tested coffee morning, but Woking Branch of the Cats Protection League is now making up for lost time. Some of these prestigious events take place in homes with wallpaper and curtains that are not held together with staples and sellotape. Others take place in my house. The cats, far from being intimidated, rather enjoy these bunfights and are anxious to show people round, particularly if there is a headless mouse or mummified frog to be admired.

Then there is the paws-on cat rescue, which is about a great deal more than fostering and rehoming. There are any number of feral or wild cats that are always needing trapping, neutering and feeding, and these will receive our undivided atention in the next chapter. A lot of time is also spent on helping the elderly and infirm to get their cats to the vet, or in clipping claws and administering worm pills, or in giving financial assistance to those who are unable to meet their vet's bills.

Fostering and rehoming has its stressful side, not because of the cats and kittens, but because some ghastlies are bound to be encountered along the way. I often think that stress levels would fall if only we weren't encumbered with all this civilisation nonsense which makes us hesitate to tell a ghastly about his or her shortcomings in a helpful and totally unambiguous way. However, when taking in a pussycat from a bad home it is best to hold back until Fluffy is safely incarcerated in the cat carrier and one is within striking distance of the door.

I still treasure fond memories of the ghastly who called me out on Boxing Day to collect a little cat which was, apparently, 'shitting all over me carpet and costing a fortune.' When I arrived at the second floor flat I discovered a tiny white and tabby kitten with a neck like raw meat where it had ripped itself to pieces. Wading between mobile phones, video recorders and computers, but not dirt trays, I captured 'Charlie' and departed with the ghastly's exhortations ringing in my ears: 'You mind you look after 'im! 'E's 'ad the best of everything! I've treated 'im like me own flesh and blood!'

Some cats, of course, come in for rehoming for the saddest of reasons. It might be that an elderly owner has had to go into a home where pets are not allowed. Sometimes a baby will have a violent allergic reaction to the cat (and often the cat will have a violent reaction to the baby if things haven't been handled properly!).

The really rewarding side of this activity is seeing the cat comfortably settled in its new home. The sight of Fluffy, or Tigger, or Patch, spreadeagled across the owner's knee, quite unable to think who this batty woman is gives the fosterer a real boost, although it can be tricky if the owner doesn't recognise her either.

Cat fosterers commonly suffer from a disease known as Incremental Cat Acquisition (ICA) which manifests itself in the sudden and mysterious growth of their feline families. How can it be, you might ask, that a perfectly rational person with two cats, within a matter of months becomes a totally irrational person with six cats? As yet there is little to indicate that the NHS is taking the condition at all seriously.

Appended to this chapter is an essential glossary of well known cat rescuer phrases which the beginner may find helpful.

CAT RESCUER PHRASES

ESSENTIAL GLOSSARY

Cat Rescuer Phrase	Translation
I'm not sure of her exact age	She won't see 12 again
He's not really used to children	Count their fingers before leaving
She's not all that keen on cat food	You might get away with pink salmon, but probably not
He loves dogs	Braised, grilled or curried
She's not the best traveller in the world	She'll scream and pooh all the way
He's particularly loving	Don't expect to ever have the bed to yourself again
Just 5 minutes' grooming a day should do it	Set aside 5 hours
He hasn't been used to a pussyflap	Prepare to spend the next 6 months on your hands and knees
She'd probably do best as an only cat	She'll kill any cat within a 5-mile radius

He loves dogs..........

Cat Rescuer Phrase	Translation
She's a cat for the connoisseur	You'd have to be a real cat freak to put up with this one
He tends to nip if he's frightened	If **HE'S** frightened......?
Insecurity can manifest itself in all sorts of ways	Stock up on carpet cleaner
She's had to fend for herself up to now	How are you with mice and worms?
Once he trusts you, you'll be the centre of his furry little universe	How much do you value being alone in the bathroom?
She can be difficult with tablets	Contact the SAS at worm pill time
He's what I'd describe as 'chatty'	You won't be able to hear yourself think
She's a sensitive little cat	Upset this one and your life won't be worth living

CHAPTER EIGHT

THERE ARE FURRIES AT THE BOTTOM OF MY GARDEN

There are wild cats everywhere. Not wild by species, of course, but domestic cats that have run wild - and have usually made a very thorough job of it.

In some situations this might not be a problem, either for the cats or for that other rather prolific species, the human being. Most cat rescuers are not obsessed with taming every cat they clap eyes on, but the sad truth is that most of present day Britain does not offer a very hospitable environment to the wild, or feral, cat. Most cats that run wild end up on the streets because this is where they have been dumped or abandoned when owners move away. They are far more likely to be skulking in a back alley in Basildon than playing prettily in a sunlit glade surrounded by plentiful supplies of suicidal rodents.

Cats that have been dumped by our old friends the ghastlies are unlikely to have been spayed or castrated, and - given the cat's propensity for indulging in hanky panky - the outcome is all too predictable: litter after litter of sickly kittens which will in turn breed with each other so that a relatively minor difficulty escalates into a major disaster in no time at all.

Many people who contact cat rescue organisations about feral cats only do so when they become aware

The cat person about to do battle

that the skulking shadow in their garden is becoming more bulky than skulky. It is at this point that the cat person sets off with traps, gauntlets and pilchards to do battle with Fluffy and any of Fluffy's friends that fancy joining in.

Over the years my respect for the wildies has increased, as has my cowardice. I am convinced there is nothing braver or wilder than a feral cat, which can make a fox seem quite cuddly by comparison. Ferals are generally stronger than a domestic cat of similar proportions, and because they are fighting for their lives when cornered they tend to have strong views on being handled. The simplest way to catch them is a humane trap, suitably positioned and baited with something really scrummy. The downside of this activity is that the cat trapper's car – and probably her person – will at best reek of pilchards and at worst a heady blend of pilchards and cat urine well into the next century.

Some wildies refuse to co-operate, however, and other 'hands-on' methods may be called for. Sometimes Mrs Thingy will have struck up a relationship with the furry shadow and it may be possible to lure the cat into a conservatory or similar structure so that the cat rescuer can catch it.

Mrs Thingy will either wonder what all the fuss is about and chuckle as gauntlets are donned, or will become hopelessly emotional and convinced that poor Fluffy's legs will snap as you wrestle her into a cat carrier. A further challenge can often be presented by the nature of the conservatory which is likely to be jam-packed with geraniums, garden furniture and, for some reason best known to Mrs Thingy, priceless antique vases. It is, regrettably, unusual for a feral cat to come out with its paws up; it is also unlikely that the cat rescuer, falling some way short of Olympic standards, will succeed in grabbing and holding on to Fluffy at the first pass. There is, therefore, almost bound to be a fairly tense interlude during which the hunter and the hunted will weigh up each other's capabilities and during which Mrs Thingy will get in the way, weep, or vow she could have managed the whole thing better herself.

Cat rescuers would be well-advised to keep quiet at this stage, not just out of politeness, but because they will need every scrap of breath they can force into their lungs once the chase starts in earnest.

Generally the aim will be to have the cat neutered and then return him or her to the scene of the abduction as long as feeding can be arranged on a fairly regular basis, and as long as the territory is reasonably safe. Sometimes, however, returning Fluffy is not a viable option, either because Mrs Thingy is adamant that she will poison the cat if it dares to darken her azalea bush again, or because the site is about to be demolished, etc., etc.

In theory, relocating a feral cat or cats to a suitable site sounds easy. In practice, it is almost impossible to achieve in most areas of the country. The ideal target would appear to be a farm or smallholding, but in reality most farmers who are well-disposed towards cats have already got them and the other sort are inclined to view as vermin anything that can't be served up with a sprig of rosemary.

Not every cat that is referred as a wildie turns out to be the genuine article, of course. I answered the phone one evening to a tearful woman who was convinced that the 'monster' at the bottom of her garden was about to dismember not only her cat, but her and her husband also. I wasted no time in turning out to trap the brute. It was exceedingly dark in the garden and colder than any evening has a right to be. I could hear the patter of not-so-tiny paws in the undergrowth and baited the trap with trembling hands. I hardly had time to step to one side before the 'wild beast' hurled himself into the trap with an audible sigh of relief. 'Thank goodness you've come! He purred. 'It's been hell out here.'

I have a soft spot for wildies. After all, we owe them something, having lured the original wild cats into our homes. If the human race had played fair with them and taken its responsibilities seriously there wouldn't be so many dispossessed felines grappling for a pawhold in our towns and suburbs.

Several of my cats are ex-wildies, including Lucy and Brocky who were trapped on the railway embankment when Lucy was heavily pregnant. Lucy was trapped first and poor Brocky all but battered his way in, panic at being left alone rendering him vulnerable to the rescuers. By the time Lucy had reared her kittens we were worried about returning them to the embankment, where broken bottles and beer cans were a great deal more plentiful than plates of Kittydins, and so they remained in our care.

One sunny morning I opened the door of their pen and retreated. Brocky soon emerged, walked the few feet he had been used to walking then, realising there was no barrier, scaled the back fence and disappeared into the woods. Lucy, always the wiser of the two, waited until nightfall before setting off to find her son (and possibly her husband!). There was no sign of either cat next morning and my exultation at setting them free was rapidly giving way to tearful anxiety.

After much plate banging, a familiar black and white face appeared over the fence. Yes, Brocky had returned. A few seconds later, a smaller black and white figure joined him. Lucy had come home.

Lucy and Brocky have long since joined the gang that sleep on the bed at night, only the occasional fleeting nervousness betraying their feral origins. I currently have three wild boys who live outside, but there are already indications that Tufty is considering renting space on the sofa, and I have caught Dennis showing an anything but feral interest in 'Coronation Street' once or twice when the patio door has been open.

Feral cats ask very little – regular feeding and some shelter from the elements, in return for which the cat lover can have his or her own miniature safari park. The one thing to bear in mind is that you can't really rely on wildies staying wild; there is every prospect that the furries at the bottom of your garden will in due course become the furries sprawled across your duvet.

CHAPTER NINE

BECOMING AN EXPERT

We all know about cats being creatures of mystery and witchiness, but for my money the strangest phenomenon of all is the effect they have on human beings. Far from gaining knowledge as the years go by, the cat person invariably finds that he or she knows less and less, until after ten years or so the poor soul can barely distinguish a white cat from a black one or a Persian from a Sphinx.

It's not that the cat expert doesn't know the answers. In a darkened, cat-free room the answers would no doubt follow as night follows day. No, it's the way that cats look at you that does it: that cool and slightly contemptuous stare which has the human wondering whether there is something suspect on at least one shoe.

My heart sinks when I answer the phone and an anxious voice says, 'My friend said I should speak to you. She said you'd know why Suki has started to.......' It is very flattering to be asked, but I suspect the man on the proverbial Clapham omnibus would be a more valuable source of information on many occasions. For, in common with most cat rescuers, I have my secrets.

One of my darkest secrets concerns Derek, a chubby blue-grey cat who arrived with his slightly dotty owners one murky autumn night. These people were not ghastlies, but the effects of their well-meaning bumbling were still pretty disastrous. They arrived with three cats, none of which were in cat carriers 'because they don't like being confined'. I suggested that the owners should bring the cats through to the pens, one at a time, weariness and a desperate awareness that whatever we did the cats were likely to end up legging it clouding my thinking. Two cats were safely transferred, and Mrs Dilly was all but inside the pen with Derek when he flung himself across the garden and over the back fence.

I am not proud of the names I called the Dillys, but suffice it to say that the point was made and they spent a very uncomfortable couple of hours searching for poor Derek in a dark and scratchy whirlpool of brambles and bracken. Come to that, so did I, but I deserved to because I also had let Derek down badly. At last we abandoned the hunt and the Dillys drove off with a cheery wave, promising to return in the morning to bring him back from the woods.

Just after 7am Mrs Dilly's inimitable 'cooee!' reverberated through the letterbox. I hadn't slept well, having made numerous excursions into the frosty darkness in a forlorn attempt to retrieve young Derek, and I have a vague recollection that I may have snapped as I handed her the cat carrier. I think I may even have mumbled something like, 'If you fondly imagine, Mrs Dilly, that the cat will still be sitting there ten hours later, you're in for a shock, I can assure you!'

Ten minutes later the doorbell jangled and there was Mrs Dilly – and there inside the carrier was Derek.

Another legendary error of judgement on my part concerned Fluffy, who came in for rehoming after her elderly owner had been admitted to a nursing home. Now I have to say that Fluffy was not the most prepossessing of pussycats, being rather slow to see the joke and rather quick to lash out at the old ankles when one visited her. I soon began to realise why her owner's son had made such a generous donation to our funds. The months went by, various potential owners were introduced to Fluffy, and left with apologies, TCP and plasters.

After eight months I was at my wits' end and was self-indulgently rambling away to a friend of mine who has two young children and two other cats when I suddenly realised she was saying something significant. 'Perhaps we could take Fluffy,' she said in a calm voice. 'We could give it a try anyway.'

My feeble protests were swept to one side and we all trooped in to visit Madam in her boudoir. I closed my eyes as the boy stuck his face within an inch of Fluffy's grizzled muzzle. When I opened them again it was to see Fluffy rolling over, her thin legs waving in the air and there was a very strange noise emanating from her direction. Yes, the old tart was purring and yes – she has lived happily with them ever since.

On another occasion I took in three cats for rehoming, all of uncertain age and extremely unlikely to see twelve again. Within two days I received a call from a pleasant-sounding family who were interested in taking on an older cat. Round they came and were instantly smitten by the pretty little tabby member of the trio. As I started to make arrangements for taking the tabby round to them, I became aware of significant looks passing between the parents. I asked if there was anything I could help with. 'Well – we hardly like to ask really. I mean, it's a bit of a cheek. It's just that we wondered if you'd consider letting us have all three – it seems such a shame to split them, doesn't it?' It was a golden moment, a moment to be savoured and weighed in the balance the very next time a ghastly told me to do the biologically impossible.

Most people who spend a lot of time around cats become quite adept at distinguishing boys from girls and neutered boys from entire toms, but every now and then, usually when one is feeling rather smug about things, an error creeps in, as in the case of little Twinkle. Twinkle was about two years old and exceedingly furry. 'He' was a stray and in my defence I would add that Twinkle was not at all keen on liberties being taken with 'his' person. A quick feel while his attention was being diverted by a plate of sardines revealed two distinct bulges in the nether regions, and before the sun had set little Twinkle was booked in for castration. Imagine my confusion when I collected Twinkle and was informed that his 'male assets' were actually two unfortunately positioned knots of fur. Still, vets have stressful lives and I was pleased to provide them with a rare moment of relaxation, even if it was at my expense.

Thankfully, being wrong about cats isn't confined to the batty catty population: vets sometimes suffer from it too. After spending a lively half-hour chasing a sparky tabby girl around the pen, I finally cornered her and whisked her off to the vet's to have the stitches removed following her spay operation. I blurted out the whole sordid tale of how difficult she'd been, to be confronted with a knowing smile and a nonchalant wave of the hand. 'She'll be fine if we don't crowd her,' he said. 'Just open the door of the carrier and let her come out at her own speed.' Grave misgivings beset me at this point, but I did as I was bid. 'Her own speed' was approximately 90mph and it took the two of us a good 20 minutes to catch her by flinging a blanket over her. We then had to call in two nurses to help while the stitches were removed. That little cat weighed no more than 6lbs. Makes you think, doesn't it?

Another strange thing about cat rescuers is our total inability to learn from past mistakes. Only the other day I was exhorting a rather nervous couple to make sure their cat knew who was boss – just as dear Miss Amber swiped me smartly across the knuckles because she thought it was way past supper time.

There is, of course, endless scope for making a fool of yourself when you are frequently called upon to clip claws and administer worm pills. I was just congratulating myself on having successfully rammed a pill down little Kitty's throat when the spirited creature twisted round and ripped my blouse, spitting out the pill in the same fluid movement. I was so intent on getting the medication down her that I didn't notice my *deshabille* until the battle was won, but thankfully one can rely on Damart not to reveal all.

Time and time again heartbroken old ladies parting with a much-loved cat in tragic circumstances will tell me that Cindy will only eat fish, or that Basil must go to an indoor home because he hates going outside, and that Smokey loves being groomed. So why is it that before the car bringing them has rounded the corner Cindy is demanding a rare steak, Basil wants nothing more than to rush into the woods, and Smokey has all but had my hand off as I reach for her favourite brushy-wushy?

And there was naughty little Pansy, who flirted outrageously with every boy cat she clapped her limpid eyes on, then set about killing poor Teddy who was besotted with his pretty tortoiseshell companion. It all worked out in the end, but only after their owners had bought a bigger house so that the cats would have more space and little Pansy wouldn't feel 'threatened'.

Yes, the sad truth is that cats just won't respect expertise, even if it is packaged in a white coat. In fact, the only thing you can ever be sure of is their total unpredictability.

Cats don't always take to a new companion

There are a number of survival strategies.....

CHAPTER TEN

SURVIVAL STRATEGIES

Sometimes it takes years for the innocent, untested cat person encountered in Chapter One to turn into the eccentric, haunted creature described in the last few pages. Sometimes it happens almost overnight, but however long it takes, happen it will given even the smallest chink in that human armour generally referred to as commonsense or self-preservation.

Along the way the person often makes remarks like, 'I am in control of my life,' or, 'of course the tail isn't wagging the dog!' This is usually while they are waiting for treatment at the local Accident and Emergency Department, nursing at least one broken limb under their ketchup-spattered clothing.

Most cat people retain enough sense to admit defeat fairly early on, realising that they are in the presence of a superior and ruthless intelligence. Leaving aside the obvious comforts afforded by chocolate and alcohol, there are a number of survival strategies which can help to make life bearable.

Excelling at Amateur Dramatics

Even the quietest of cats has a pronounced taste for the melodramatic and will respect the development of dramatic qualities in its human. Some cats love to sing and the uninhibited participation of the human in a rousing rendering of 'Danny Boy' will earn him or her some much needed, if grudging, admiration.

On a more practical level, the ability to convey to a cat that nothing could be further from one's mind than catching it, ramming it into a cat carrier and rushing it off to the vet's, is beyond price. A high level of skill is needed. Simply walking towards Cat 1 when the real target is Cat 2 will fool nobody. Oh, no – a far more sophisticated approach is called for, probably involving an overhead crane, safety nets and Shakespearean costumes.

With the administration of pills, some owners have become such devotees of the Method School of Acting that they have themselves ingested a dangerous level of medication. Still, every cloud has a silver lining, and at least they are unlikely to suffer from tapeworm infestation or other unpleasant maladies.

Coping with Allegations of Eccentricity

We all know that anti-cat people like nothing better than to foster an image of the cat lover as a sad person with an empty life. Now this is just silly. There must be some people with cats who are leading more or less normal lives – aren't there?

Anyway, in order to refute these cruel allegations it sometimes becomes necessary to do something undeniably and flamboyantly normal, such as cleaning the windows, or mowing the lawn. It might even be advisable to occasionally be seen buying something other than cat food, gin and Milk Tray at the supermarket.

Being Brazen

It doesn't do to think apologising for being a cat person is always the answer, because sometimes it can actually work in the cat lover's favour. I once went for a job interview, only to be greeted with the encouraging news that the response to the advertisement had been amazing and the quality of those interviewed so far beyond belief. As I faced the panel I was aghast to see that the gleaming navy newness of my new M & S skirt was concealed beneath a blanket of cat fur. Far from ruining my chances, however, my nervous smoothing of George's tabby trimmings proved my salvation. I might not have known anything about computers and even less about budgeting, but what my future boss really wanted to know was how and when to worm little Bobby. And they worry about Freemasonry!

The Cat Lover's Vet

The serious cat person will naturally be concerned about choosing the right vet, not just because he or she wants the best for the furry family, but because many hours are likely to be spent in the waiting room and surgery. What most cat lovers cannot abide is a flippant attitude to Fluffy's phantom pregnancy, or muffled hysteria when Sammy's anal glands are under discussion. No, a certain professional gravitas is called for, plus considerable athletic ability to cope with Sammy's entirely understandable reluctance to have his problem investigated.

A common problem is that with the passing of the years, the cat person is likely to gather into the fold cats of mature years, and it can be a worrying thing to find that the vet is junior by some years to one's cat. Most cats are quite good about this sort of thing, as long as the person in the white coat has warm hands.

Making Sure People Know It Could Be Worse

If a cat person does begin to feel under seige because of the number of felines on the premises, it can be a useful ploy to hint that something much larger, or fiercer, or noisier is on the way. A few library books on 'Hand Rearing Lions' or 'Keeping Poisonous Snakes' could result in friends and neighbours being pathetically grateful that they've only got Bubbles, Montgomery, Annabelle, Plato and Tootsie to contend with.

Another useful trick is to put the house on the market and encourage a friend to call round with a car load of children and dogs – all borrowed if necessary. If things really go well the neighbours could end up pleading with the cat owner to stay.

And if All Else Fails...........

As the cat lover clings to the edge of the bed, or crouches on the floor so as not to disturb Tigger, or Linus, or Poppy, or Titania, there is some small consolation in knowing that exactly the same thing is happening in millions of other homes across the world. There is evidence to indicate that pussy people everywhere are emerging from their closets, removing their dark glasses and standing tall – well, as tall as they can after humping tons of cat litter and Kittydins for the greater part of their lives. And as they stand, blinking in the brilliant dawn of a New Cat Age, Kitty and Fluffy, Bramble and Patch, are wondering just how long it will be before they all pull themselves together and get their breakfast dished up.

WHAT CATS THINK ABOUT HUMANS

An extensive survey of feline views has revealed what Fluffy and her friends think about us and the way we live. Some of the more printable comments appear below:

Q: What do you think of the way your human dresses?

A: I'm just thankful that she wears clothes, having accidentally caught sight of her in the bath the other evening.

I've never seen her in a dress. She usually wears baggy trousers or, even worse, leggings. Leggings should be banned in my opinion – at least for people over five months of age.

He only seems to have one suit and unfortunately it suffered rather in my last outbreak of tail-end squitters. He looks best when he's dishing up my Kittydins and worst when he's manhandling me into the cat carrier.

You should have seen her when she went off to that wedding! Talk about done up like a cat's supper! Ouch!

Q: What sort of job does your human do?

A: A pretty simple one I should think, judging by the problems she has getting the clothes out of the washing machine.

He's always telling people how important he is, but I've seen him screwing up balls of paper. He's much too lazy to run after them though.

I think she's something called a pussonnel officer and she does a lot of intermewing.

I don't know what she does and I don't care. The important thing is that it gets her out from under my paws for a few hours a day.

She works in a greengrocers. Whatever use is that?

Q: Would you say your human is the sporty type?

A: Are we talking about the same person?

He fancies his chances as another Paul Gascoigne, which is just as well because nobody else does.

She used to go jogging, but then there was that nasty episode with a Rottweiler and she gave it up. The dog's recovering well now.

No and I don't want her to be. One bad sprain and where does that leave the tin opener, answer me that!

Q: What's the strangest thing your human does?

A: Every morning he scrapes his face with a metal thing, but luckily he hasn't tried it on me yet. Mind you, his fur is so tacky, it's probably best to get rid of it.

She's obsessed with the garden and spends hours pulling up some flowers and putting in others. When I tried to help her, she got very excited but I heard her tell somebody she was at a 'funny age'. It might be funny for her, but it's no joke from where I'm standing.

She spends hours talking on the phone and sometimes she doesn't mention me for ten seconds at a time.

She's convinced she can drive.

Q: **What's your human's favourite bedtime reading?**

A: 'Tapeworm in the Older Cat'

'Life Without Cats'

'Coping With Furballs'

'Introducing A New Cat Or Kitten' – Oh, no!

Q: **Does your human always put you first?**

A: What a strange question!

I'm sure he does because that new girlfriend hasn't been back after I made my views clear. How was I to know it was a new skirt?

She's inclined to be selfish, but a bit of projectile vomiting usually focuses her mind.

Of course she does. I'm here, aren't I?

Q: **If you could change one thing about your human, what would it be?**

A: You've got me there! I wouldn't know where to start!

I wish she didn't think she could sing. How would you like to wake up with 'Kiri's Karaoke'?

His knees. They're so bony.

I don't see why she has to take up so much room in bed.

Q: What do you love best about your human?

A: She's very overweight and has a large lap.

She's not very bright.

He dotes on me.

Well – I'll have to think about that. I mean, she's not too bad on a good day, but there again.......

INGRATITUDE REDEFINED

His long fur matted, one leg lame,
    The tabby cat without a name
Would ransack dustbins, wolf down crusts,
    Curl up in cobwebs, dream in dust.

The weeks went by. His old coat shone;
    He basked now in a kinder sun.
Taking time to savour meals,
    He now preferred his shellfish peeled.

On cold nights now he hogs the bed
    And lets me kiss his gleaming head,
But sadly when it's warm and fine
    His tabby heart's no longer mine.

The woods will call him and the stream,
    The stars, the great moon's silvery beam;
He has so much to do, you see,
    He cannot waste his time with me.

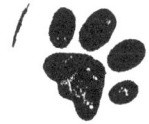

AUTHOR'S NOTE

I should love to hear from anyone who can help me to write about anything other than cats. I'm not fussy - mountain bikes, embroidery, car maintenance - it really would be a relief to get my mind on to something else.

I often start to write what should turn out to be a blockbuster - a real bodice-ripper, but before my hero has closed the bedroom door he will have turned into Malcolm, or Brocky, or even dear old Sammy-Cat, and he'll be squaring up to Miss Amber, not for some steamy hanky-panky, but for half a pilchard or a lump of chicken.

I have the same problem when I read a book. I love a good murder mystery, but Inspector Morse will always look like a grumpy old Persian to me and Lewis a good natured British Blue. When I watch 'Brief Encounter' it is always Trevor-the-Tom sharing a saucer of milk with Celia-Slinky-Paws, and if I encounter a village cricket match in my travels it could only be my own dear Malcolm at the crease.

I recently took on an ancient ginger cat who soon became 'Captain Mainwaring' because of his general air of bossiness and flair for being totally wrong about almost everything. The strange thing is that although the cat was originally named after the legendary 'Dad's Army' character, whenever I watch repeats of that wonderful series I seem to see not dear Arthur Lowe, but a whiskery - and decidedly feline - countenance.

I am not helped, of course, by the people who write long and lovely letters to Malcolm - people who are obviously suffering from the same Furryphile syndrome and encourage me in my descent into battiness. I used to worry whether they would find out about my problem at work, but luckily I seem to have cracked that one.

Forget about becoming normal. Most of us have left it far too late for that and the strain would finish us. The answer is to bring everybody else down to the same level of lunacy. A colleague of mine keeps horses and we have wonderful conversations with her doing horse voices and me chattering away in pussy language. A non-petowning person who shares our office has a teddy bear – a rather petulant character who complains loudly about people who haven't made a cup of tea for ages, or ate all the biscuits while the rest of us were at a meeting.

So, forget about being normal, let's hear it for the twilight world. There are worse things in life than love and laughter – Malcolm said so.